Contents

Hi, I'm Ben.

Welcome to my farm.

My Farm

My Pigs

by Heather Miller

SCHOLASTIC INC.

New York Toronto London Auckland Sydney
Mexico City New Delhi Hong Kong Buenos Aires

Photo Credits: cover, pp. 5, 7, 11, 13, 15, 17, 19 by Jeffrey Foxx; p. 9 © Index Stock; p. 21 © Michele Burgess/Index Stock

Contributing Editor: Jennifer Ceaser
Book Design: Michael DeLisio

ISBN 0-516-23883-3

12 11 10   5 6 7/0

Printed in the U.S.A.   10

First Scholastic printing, March 2002

5

This is my pig, Pinky.

Pinky comes when I call her by name.

"Here Pinky!"

We also have a **sow** on our farm.

A sow is a mother pig.

Her babies are called **piglets**.

9

Fred is our **boar**.

A boar is a father pig.

A boar is bigger than a sow.

Do you like to eat corn for breakfast?

Pigs do.

Pinky **grunts** as she eats.

It is a very hot day.

How do my pigs stay cool?

They lie in the mud.

14

15

Night is coming.

I feed my pigs one more time.

17

My pigs go to the **trough** to drink water.

Then it is time for them to go into their **pens**.

Goodnight, my pigs!

21

New Words

boar (**bor**) a father pig

grunts (**gruntz**) sounds a pig makes

pens (**penz**) areas where pigs sleep

piglets (**pig**-letz) baby pigs

sow (**sow**) a mother pig

trough (**trawf**) a long box that holds
water or food

To Find Out More

Web Site
Barnyard Buddies
http://www.execpc.com/~byb/
Meet the Barnyard Buddies. Learn more about farm animals.
Includes games and posters to color. E-mail your favorite animal!